THE NATIONAL POETRY SERIES

Tenth Annual Series—1989

Emily Hiestand, *Green the Witch Hazel Wood*
(Selected by Jorie Graham)

David Mura, *After We Lost Our Way*
(Selected by Gerald Stern)

Len Roberts, *Black Wings*
(Selected by Sharon Olds)

Lee Upton, *No Mercy*
(Selected by James Tate)

Paul Zimmer, *The Great Bird of Love*
(Selected by William Stafford)

The National Poetry Series was established in 1978 to publish five collections of poetry annually through five participating publishers. The manuscripts are selected by five poets of national reputation. Publication is funded by the Copernicus Society of America, James A. Michener, Edward J. Piszek, the Lannan Foundation, the Friends of the National Poetry Series, and the five publishers—the Atlantic Monthly Press, E. P. Dutton, Graywolf Press, Persea Books, and the University of Illinois Press.

AFTER WE LOST OUR WAY

ALSO BY DAVID MURA

A Male Grief: Notes on Pornography & Addiction

DAVID MURA

AFTER WE LOST OUR WAY

THE NATIONAL POETRY SERIES
SELECTED BY GERALD STERN

E. P. DUTTON  NEW YORK

 ☐ Published in the United States by E. P. Dutton, a division of NAL Penguin Inc., 2 Park Avenue, New York, N.Y. 10016. ☐ Published simultaneously in Canada by Fitzhenry and Whiteside, Limited, Toronto. ☐ Library of Congress Cataloging-in-Publication Data ☐ Mura, David. ☐ After we lost our way / David Mura. ☐ p. cm. — (The National poetry series) ☐ ISBN 0-525-24758-0. — ISBN 0-525-48483-3 (pbk.) ☐ I. Title. II. Series. ☐ PS3563.U68A35 1989 ☐ 811'.54—dc19 ☐ Designed by Earl Tidwell ☐ 1 2 3 4 5 6 7 8 9 10 ☐ First Edition.

Some of the poems in this book appeared, in slightly different versions, in the following magazines and anthologies:

The American Poetry Review: "The Natives," "Lan Nguyen: The Uniform of Death (1971)," "Grandfather-in-Law"
Another Chicago Magazine: "Suite for Grandfather & Grandmother Uyemura: Relocation"
Crazyhorse: "The Emergency Room," "Nantucket Honeymoon"
Fallout: "Huy Nguyen: Brothers, Drowning Cries"
Great River Review: "Elegy for a Poet"
The Indiana Review: "This Loss, This Brightness," "The One Who Tells, The One Who Burns," "The Architect's Son," "*These Years Are Obscure, Their Chronicle Uncertain*"
Kyoto Review: "Song for Uncle Tom, Tonto and Mr. Moto"
The Missouri Review: "Letters from Poston Relocation Camp (1942–45)"
The Nation: "Grandfather and Grandmother in Love"
The New Republic: "From the Pages of *Corriere della Sera* (Oct. 29, 1975): A Lutheran Letter"

The following poems were reprinted in *Breaking Silence: An Anthology of Contemporary Asian-American Poets* (The Greenfield Review Press, 1983): "The *Hibakusha*'s Letter (1955)," "A *Nisei* Picnic: From An Album," "The Natives," "Lan Nguyen: The Uniform of Death (1971)," and "Huy Nguyen: Brothers, Drowning Cries."

Reprinted in *An Ear to the Ground* (University of Georgia Press, 1989) were: "Lost in the Philippines," "The Natives," "Grandfather and Grandmother in Love," and "Nantucket Honeymoon."

"The Bookstore" first appeared in *Milkweed Chronicle* and was reprinted in *The Utne Reader* and *A Male Grief: Notes on Pornography & Addiction* (Milkweed Editions, 1987).

"Huy Nguyen: Brothers, Drowning Cries" and "The Natives" were reprinted in *Carrying the Darkness: The Poetry of the Vietnam War* (Avon Books, 1985).

“Song for Uncle Tom, Tonto and Mr. Moto,” “The *Hibakusha*’s Letter (1955),” “The Natives,” and “Huy Nguyen: Brothers, Drowning Cries” were reprinted in *Minnesota Writes: Poetry* (Milkweed Editions, 1987).

Some of the passages in “Pasolini” are adapted from Norman MacAffee’s notes to his translation, *Pier Paolo Pasolini: Poems* (Vintage Books, 1982); *Pier Paolo Pasolini: Lutheran Letters,* translated by Stuart Hood (Carcanet Press, 1987); or *Pier Paolo Pasolini* by Pia Friedrich (Copyright © 1982. Reprinted with the permission of Twayne Publishers, a division of G. K. Hall & Co., Boston).

The epigraphs to the four sections are from the following sources:
Minima Moralia, Theodor Adorno (Verso Editions, 1978)
The Human Province, Elias Canetti (The Seabury Press, 1978)
Illuminations, Walter Benjamin (Shocken Books, 1969)

ACKNOWLEDGMENTS

I would like to express my deepest gratitude and thanks to the following people for their support: James Moore, Deborah Keenan, J. P. White, Patricia Kirkpatrick, Susan Swanson, Sheila Murphy, David Wojahn, and Donald Hall.

I also would like to thank my parents, Tom and Teruko Mura, and my father-in-law and mother-in-law, David and Jane Sencer, for their help and encouragement over the years.

Finally, I want to thank the following organizations for their generous assistance: The Bush Foundation, The McKnight Foundation, The Loft, The National Endowment for the Arts, The Japan–United States Friendship Commission, The Minnesota State Arts Board, The Center for Arts Criticism.

For Susie

for going the long hard way with me

CONTENTS

I

II

Pasolini

III

IV

I

Nothing that has ever happened
should be regarded as lost for history.

—WALTER BENJAMIN

GRANDFATHER AND GRANDMOTHER IN LOVE

Now I will ask for one true word beyond
betrayal, that creaks and buoys like the bedsprings
used by the bodies that begot the bodies that begot me.
Now I will think of the moon bluing the white
sheets soaked in sweat, that heard him whisper
haiku of clover, azalea, the cry of the cuckoo;
complaints of moles and beetles,
blight and bad debts, as the *biwa*'s spirit
bubbled up between them, its song quavering.
Now I take this word, crack it, like a seed
between the teeth, spit it out in the world
to root in the loam of his greenhouse roses;
let it leave the sweet taste of *teriyaki,*
a grain of her rice lodged in my molars;
in my nostrils, a faint hot breath of *sake*.

Now as *otoo-san, okaa-san,* drift towards
each other, there reverberates the *ran*
of lovers, and the ship of the past bursts
into that other world; and she, still teasing,
pushes him away, swats his hand, a pesky,
tickling fly, then turns to his face that
cries out laughing, as he hauls her in,
trawling the currents, gathering
a sea that seems endless, depths a boy dreams of,
where flounder, dolphin, fluorescent fins, fish
with wings spill before him glittering scales,
and letting slip the net, he dives under,
and night washes over them, slipping from
sight, just the soft shush of waves, drifting ground
swells, echoing the knocking tide of morning.

THE *HIBAKUSHA*'S LETTER (1955)

Survivors of the atomic bomb were called hibakusha. *This name became associated with keloids, a whitish-yellow scar tissue, and later, with defects, disease, and disgrace.*

The fields, Teruko-san, are threshed. A good
Harvest. All week I've seen farmers with torches
Bend to earth, releasing fires. The winds
Sweep ash across the roads, dirty my laundry

Hung on the fence. Prayer drums, gongs, clap
In the streets, and now the village celebrates.
Last night Matsuo told me how he emptied
On a clump of rags beside the inn. Suddenly

The clump jumped up, groggy, wet, cursing.
Matsuo finished, bowed, offered him a drink.
This morning I shuffled out back to gossip
With my neighbor, an eighty-year-old woman

Who prances like a mouse about her garden.
While she jabbered Matsuo cut her firewood;
Sweat poured from the scars he no longer marks.
Later I opened my shrine to its brass Buddha,

And fruit flies scattered from the bowl of plums
I'd forgotten to change. Pulled from the rubble,
Burnt at the edges, my fiancé's picture
Crumbled in my fingers. I lit him incense.

Matsuo says we can't drag each corpse behind us
Like a shadow. The eye blinks, a world's gone,
And the slow shudder at our shoulders says
We won't be back. This year I've changed my diet:

I eat only rice, *utskemono, tofu*.
Sashimi sickens me, passion for raw meat.

Sister, remember how Mother strangled chickens?
She twirled them in the air by their necks

Like a boy with a slingshot. I'd watch in horror
Their bodies twitch, hung from her fist, and cry
That Buddha kept their karma in my stomach.
Like them we had no warning. Flames filled kimonos

With limbs of ash, and I wandered past
Smoldering trolleys away from the city.
Of course you're right. We can't even play beauty
Or the taste of steel quickens our mouths.

I can't conceive, and though Matsuo says
It doesn't matter, my empty belly haunts me:
Why call myself a woman, him a man,
If on our island only ghosts can gather?

And yet, I can't deny it. There are times,
Teruko, I am happy . . .
You say *hibakusha* should band together. Here
Fewer eyes shower us in shame. I wandered

Too far: My death flashed without, not within.
I can't come back. To beg the world's forgiveness
Gains so little, and monuments mean nothing.
I can't choose your way or even Matsuo's:

"Drink, Yoshiko, *sake*'s the one surgeon
Doesn't cost or cut." This evening, past fields black
And steaming, the pitch of night soil, I'll wander
Up foothills to the first volcanic springs.

After a wind from hell, the smell of burning
Now seems sweeter than flowers . . .

LETTERS FROM POSTON RELOCATION CAMP
(1942–45)

Dear Michiko,

Do songs sound different in prison?
I think there are more spaces between the words.
I think, when the song ends, the silence
does not stop singing. I think
there is nothing but song.

Matsuo's back, his bruises almost healed,
a tooth missing. His *biwa*
comes out again with the stars, a nightly
matter. He sends his regards.

Do you get fed these putrid gray beans?
I hope you haven't swallowed too
many of them. They put my stomach
in a permanent revolt, shouting no emperor
would ever feed his people so harshly.
I agree. Let's you and I grow
skinny together. Let's keep the peace.

Any second the lights will go off.

I look around me and see many
honest men who hide their beauty
as best they can.

I think that's what the whites hate,
our beauty, the way we carry the land
and the life of plants inside us,
seedlings and fruit, the flowers
and the flush tree, fields freed of weeds.

Why can't they see the door's inside them?
If someone found an answer to that,
they'd find an answer to why
those who are hungry and cold
go off to battle to become hungrier
and colder, farther from home.

Nine o'clock. The lights all out.

—

Dear Michiko,

Did you hear it last night?
So many cries
clinging to the wind?

Not just the grinding
of tanks, rifles and mortars,
or the sound of eyelids
closing forever, but something
hungrier, colder.

I'm frightened. So many dying.
What do our complaints
about blankets or late letters
matter? Or even our dreams?

But this was more than a dream.

It came across seas
and the mountains,
it smelled of ash, a gasless flame,

and I woke this morning
still tired, irritable, unable to rise.

Later, bending to
the tomatoes, in line to mess,
trudging through the desert dust,
the sun plowing its furrows
on my neck, I thought

I heard them again. The cries.

I wanted to answer: my lips
were cracked, dry.

Michiko,
am I going crazy?
Did you hear them?

—

. . . Sometimes, Michiko,
I think of my greenhouse,
how I used to stand at night in its fleshy,
steaming dark and say, "These are the most
beautiful orchids and roses in the world."
And their fragrance seeped inside me,
stayed even when I sold them.

What is it like now in Tokyo?
They say it has
sunk like a great ship.

Forgive me. Blessed
with a chance to talk to my wife,
more beautiful than any greenhouse rose,

all I can do is moan.
And yet, if I didn't tell you,
I would be angry at you for not listening,
blaming you for what I haven't spoken.

And it's too late for that . . .

When you write back, please
tell me what country I'm in.

I feel so poor now.
These words are all I own.

AN ARGUMENT: ON 1942

FOR MY MOTHER

Near Rose's Chop Suey and Jinosuke's grocery,
the temple where incense hovered and inspired
dense evening chants (prayers for Buddha's mercy,
colorless and deep), that day he was fired . . .

—No, no, no, she tells me. Why bring it back?
The camps are over. (Also overly dramatic.)
Forget *shoyu*-stained *furoshiki, mochi* on a stick:
You're like a terrier, David, gnawing a bone, an old, old trick . . .

Mostly we were bored. Women cooked and sewed,
men played blackjack, dug gardens, a *benjo.*
Who noticed barbed wire, guards in the towers?
We were children, hunting stones, birds, wild flowers.

Yes, Mother hid tins of *utskemono* and eel
beneath the bed. And when the last was peeled,
clamped tight her lips, growing thinner and thinner.
But cancer not the camps made her throat blacker

. . . And she didn't die then . . . after the war, in St. Paul,
you weren't even born. Oh I know, I know, it's all
part of your job, your way, but why can't you glean
how far we've come, how much I can't recall—

David, it was so long ago—how useless it seems . . .

SUITE FOR GRANDFATHER & GRANDMOTHER UYEMURA: RELOCATION

FOR MY AUNT RUTH

In 1918, as the sea sparkled like the last tear God
shed before giving up on the world, women
in kimonos, hair chignoned and black, faces
powdered pale white, lined the ship's rail like

the horizon of a planet with dozens of moons.
On that ledge where the East hurls forth pages
of rice, gongs, tiny brass idols with tiny brass bellies,
more mysterious than the Holy Ghost's whispers,

the women craned forward, giggled and grew
silent as the sea gulls squealed. Minutes later,
when these soon-to-be brides descended to
the dock, and their fate rushed toward them,

a bushy-browed dwarf, nose gnarled as a ginger
root, they burst into tears: chests heaving, their
lungs sucked in the air, and the New World
tasted of salt, how the photos had lied.

But he, he's so handsome he's fetched her
in person, holds her as America rises and falls ahead.
(Last night in their cabin, still shy, she fumbled
at his collar button; he unraveled her black silk *obi.*)

—

Two decades pass, his greenhouse hisses
with his orchids like petulant courtesans,
the eucalyptus rattles out back in the moonlight.
He's gone to Jap Town, Cuban cigar jammed

in his jaw. Putting down a swig of bourbon
he hurls the dice across the table: snake eyes.
Dawn, he's whistling down the walk;
he stumbles in roses, says hello to the thorns.

And she? Past his snores, she slips out to
sunlight, her basket of laundry brimming
with whiteness. Before the streets where her children
shoot coppers, hit homers, buy *Photoplay,*

where *hakujin*—pale ghosts—pass by
like large bobbing eggshells, she hauls up
a sheet: Her world's still *udon,*
utskemono, tea in pale green cups.

And then it's Pearl, Heart Mountain, mornings
when rifle towers, like ancient shrines,
obscure the horizon. Walking from the mess,
he creases a napkin like the nine-ply folds

of heaven: Out of his hands, flies a slim
white crane. She smiles, shakes her head,
forgets that moment, barbed wire and guards.
That night in the barracks she sees her sister's

house in Tokyo, firebombs and flames
peeling like skin the paper walls—A year later,
the war over, a letter arrives: it contains
her dream. By then she is smaller, fevered,

in a cheap hotel in Chicago. He offers her
mochi, puts his palm to her forehead.
Touches only air. When she reappears
in the blue shade of a cypress, she's saying

like a music box just opened, it's child's
play, isn't it, this living, this song? He
wakes confused, Lake Shore Drive traffic
spilling like surf through the screen. Bearing

hams, cigarettes, radios to distant relatives,
he returns to Tokyo. On *tatami,* limbs folded
with an old man's muscleless elegance
(In the garden, is it a nightingale or crow,

this black, black bird that sings?),
he thinks of a woman—he'll soon remarry—
then strokes these seventeen syllables:
bonsai tree   like me you are useless   and a little sad

A *NISEI* PICNIC: FROM AN ALBUM

Here is my uncle, a rice ball in his mouth,
a picnic basket (ants crawl in the slats) at his side.
Eventually he ballooned like Buddha,
over three hundred pounds. I used to stroke
his immense belly, which was scarred by shrapnel.
It made me feel patriotic.
Once, all night, he lay in a ditch near the Danube,
shoved in his intestines with his hands.
When he came back, he couldn't rent an apartment.
"Shikatta ga nai," he said. *Can't be helped.*

Turning from her boyfriend, a glint of giggle
caught in the shadows, my aunt never married.
On the day of her wedding, sitting in the bath,
she felt her knees lock; she couldn't get up.
For years I wanted to be her son.
She took me to zoos, movies, bought me candy.
When I grew up, she started raising minks
in her basement—"To make money," she said—
Most of them died of chills. She folded each one
in a shoebox and buried it in her yard.

My father's the one pumping his bicep.
(Sleek, untarnished, he still swims two miles a day.)
I can't claim that his gambling like his father
lost a garage, greenhouse or grocery,
or that, stumbling drunk, he tumbled in
the bushes with Mrs. Hoshizaki, staining
his tuxedo with mulberries and mud. He
worked too hard to be white. He beat his son.

Shown here, my head like a moon dwarfing my body
as I struggle to rise. Who are these grown-ups?
Why are they laughing? How can I tear
the bewilderment from their eyes?

SONG FOR UNCLE TOM, TONTO AND MR. MOTO

now I, *Kitsune,* the fox
open this song—

all the way from Shikoku and Shingu I axed the forest
laid down spikes and pounded their heads, grabbed salmon
like arrows leaping from streams, all the way from Kotchi, from Akao
and sir I want to complain of having to meet behind barbed wires
too many ghost-stricken people too many fools sir forgive me
I am the dance the drum the sneaky inscrutable body
and in each heel that stamps the dust a hundred bed lice
and a feast of fleas, mosquitoes and spiders come scurrying from my
toes
and the yellow fumes and flames that spume from my mouth
are only the spouting mystic metaphysics
of a Jap who knows at last my brothers
are creatures of adobe and Sand Creek and those who bowed massa

yes, sir, all the good niggers and the mute buffalo herds
all the torrential unconsecrated nauseating flood, each
singing the old imperial clichés—whip marks and sweat, harvest, bone
and blood
yes, we shingles, the tuberculars, the descendants of plague
we live in the monstrous sarcophagi of your white cultivated heart

and yes I'm raving, asphyxiated and incurable
and now proclaiming
I nail to my heart
and to the space between my balls
and here to the spongy dampness of my brain
something so emasculated it can only be
Witch rage and primal cohesion
an inveterate blackness
a torrential demonry
an infinite journey
from kissing ass

Isis and the Dragon, Voodoo and Hindu, Buddha and Shiva, odors of
Great Spirits
brothers, these are not hermetic, these are not easy lines
these are not thrown about without frightful black marks
or tossed in the manure of oxen as pork fat is given to the dogs
and here in my uterine mind something is cleaving, beating, growling
and in a bath of vitriol it swims and sharpens its sleepy, delirious teeth
and it is rising in Soweto, in Wounded Knee
in Savannah and savannah, in the Indonesian junk shops
and the smell of the hanged man or the *shoyu*-stained tables of *hana*
in the Andes and terrifying inner storms of the Caribbean
sordid, visionary alleys of São Paulo, the alchemical, Amazonian jungles
and we are all good niggers, good gooks and japs, good spics and rice
eaters
saying memsab, sahib, bwana, boss-san, señor, father, heartthrob oh
honored and most unceasing, oh devisor and provider of our own
obsequious, ubiquitous ugliness, which stares at you baboon-like,
banana-like
dwarf-like, tortoise-like, dirt-like, slant-eyed, kink-haired, ashen and
pansied
and brutally unredeemable, we are whirling about you, tartars of the air
all the urinating, tarantula grasping, ant multiplying, succubused,
hothouse hordes
yes, it us, it us, we, we knockee, yes, sir, massa, boss-san, we tearee
down your door!

THESE YEARS ARE OBSCURE, THEIR CHRONICLE UNCERTAIN

FOR FRANK WILDERSON

Fall: that first morning when the whippoorwill
whirls up mist from the creek, where small,
wild-lipped petals of purple, jeweled with dew,
mark the field's edge, and the cotton, budded
with tufts of terrifying whiteness, stretches out
to the horizon, the blue flames of day—And yes, they are here,
stooping and pecking, fingers like spiders scurrying
through the buds; slowly, haphazardly, tiny, prickly cuts
emerge near the knuckles, so that, as the whisp-white webs
are dropped in the sacks, a red drop may be lodged inside
like a shrunken, dispossessed tongue. I don't know
what year this is: I know, on their cheeks, slats of leech-like scars
chart a face born miles, an ocean away, an unexplained,
abandoned drumming that fills the ears and is
nowhere to be heard. As this man yawns, careful
not to pause more than a moment, something glints
in his mouth, some metal attached to horsehide strips.
And slowly I see it: Far down the field, in row after row,
in every mouth, the same song, the same note—
each breath inhaled, exhaled, reined by a bit.

. . . Hours, years, pass: There is no such thing
as time . . .

And then there are gnats, scribbling
tiny scrawls in the air overhead; a cool allusiveness
floods the woods. A bell is beaten with a stick,
as at some fire or feast, and the bodies, all down the rows,
pause, rigid as oxen (it is the fall when the crops, cut
for a crisp ballroom cloth, a kerchief or sheet,
seem primal, unqualified, endless). And even as the last

beat echoes across the fields, their souls, unleashed
like the vaporous whiteness gathered at the creek,
flow, sweep, blow through the woods, dark hoots of owls,
voodoo, bright poppies in the dark, leaving
steaming, impatient scarlet drops, leading
neither north nor south, neither to life nor death,
nor even to the eyes of history, its angel blown
by a whirlwind, far from this scene, but simply
into nothingness, silence, what no one has seen.

NANTUCKET HONEYMOON

It's easy for bees to build their combs of honey,
or apples to drop, their light absorbed, but once
only the dazzle and delirium of bodies beneath me

could sing the tirade taking my life—I was white, yes,
like the bodies I claimed—And when I wanted to say
it wasn't my nature, my will, not color, failed . . .

Since then, I've become someone I never expected.
At times I'd like to think it some great act of character
or even a miracle God was preparing, long before

I finally said: I give. *No más*. Can't take it anymore.
But no, it wasn't like that. You were entering med school,
I felt threatened, I'd been reading Menninger's *Man*

Against Himself, saw myself too often in its pages.
And looking at friends, recent marriages, soon-to-be babies,
I think it was probably just as much the times, just growing up.

I learned—how else can I say it?—to love my own sweet skin.

And now on this island of wild mustard, mist
and heather, herring gulls careening in the salty,
rackety Madaket wind, we walk the beach, party

to the triumph of the palpable and small—A conch
in your palm, my palm on your shoulder, a fork
you hold up, its lemony halibut, mousse or pâté . . .

Later, from our bed, I can see the steeple and its lights,
the full moon; your head a familiar book, bobbing
on my chest. (How far I feel from that Asian island.)

Years away our grandchildren will come here saying,
This room is where I began. And returning to Boston,
Paris or Portland, they won't know how bewildered I was,

how alone. They'll think I felt American. I was always at home.

THE NATIVES

Several months after we lost our way,
they began to appear, their quiet eyes
assuring us, their small painted legs
scurrying beside us. By then our radio
had been gutted by fungus, our captain's cheek
stunned by a single bullet; our ammo vanished
the first night we discovered our maps were useless,
our compasses a lie. (The sun and stars
seemed to reel above us.) The second week
forced us on snakes, monkeys, lizards, and toads;
we ate them raw over wet smoking fires.

Waking one morning we found a riverboat
loaded with bodies hanging in the trees
like an ox on a sling, marking the stages
of flood. One of us thought he heard the whirr
of a chopper, but it was only the monsoon
drumming the leaves, soaking our skin so damp
you felt you could peel it back to scratch
the bones of your ankle. Gradually our names
fell from our mouths, never heard again.
Nights, faces glowing, we told stories of wolves,
and the jungle seemed colder, more a home.

And then we glimpsed them, like ghosts of children
darting through the trees, the curtain of rain;
we told each other nothing, hoping they'd vanish.
But one evening the leaves parted. Slowly
they emerged and took our hands, their striped
faces dripping, looking up in wonder
at our grizzled cheeks. Stumbling like gods
without powers, we carried on our backs
what they could not carry, the rusted grenades,
the ammoless rifles, barrels clotted with flies.

They waited years before they brought us
to their village, led us in circles till
time disappeared. Now, stone still, our feet
tangled with vines, we stand by their doorway
like soft-eyed virgins in the drilling rain:
the hair on our shoulders dangles and shines.

II

The ephemeral image of harmony in which goodness basks only emphasizes more cruelly the pain of irreconcilability that it foolishly denies.

—THEODOR ADORNO

PASOLINI

1 To the Subject, No Address

In photographs, you lean on your Romeo,
sweater slipped on your shoulders, or leather
pants, leather jacket, shoes with a leather
so thin it tatters in the rain like paper,
ruined by nights of sexual stalking . . . Defiant

in interviews—"I shall continue to lead the ambiguous life"—
crazy about Marx and *terza rima,* filming the
Bogate slums of your novels, Chaucer, *Oedipus,*
Gospel, Sodom, you chatted poolside at Cannes,
lampooned fascists, slipped like a Pope through

courts of intrigue, contemplative life: How
your dialectical cuts caught the sun left
in the lemon groves! With cypress, nettles, poppies
by the roadside; bells tumbling from some monastery
to the Po; in dithyrambs of olive, pepper and hazel,

poured a peasant boy's pity, your mother's
face, Friulian dreams . . . *Far from hawk-shadows,*
green meadows, with the cries of a scavenger,
I know now this longing, this weeping, this cry,
is a simple thing—Yes, it's you, my Beatrice,

my rose, my river of light . . .

2 *Ninetto at Evening*

While he was preparing The Gospel, *Pasolini discovered the teen-age Ninetto Davoli in the Roman slums . . .*

Last night, drunk, weaving home from the café,
I stumbled, and this punk hauled me in his arms,
a Madonna of sorts, and we crashed through
the doorway, across the table, glasses
splintering on the floor, chicken bones
and a greasy stain. I asked him if he loves me.
Silence. And then laughter rocked his body,
and suddenly I was grinning too, a harlequin
gulping on a wine bottle, red slivers
running down my lips. He put on a record
and began to dance . . .

A natural actor, Ninetto played in most of Pasolini's films from The Gospel *on.*

                                        Later he shoved me
down like a drowning girl, and the bristles
of his beard brushed my spine, and his fingers
slipped through my sphincter's flower, formed
a fist which ground me open, dug for organs
hidden like diamonds. Feeling myself pound,
twist and plead, jammed round his wrists, I
stared past the boundary where beauty starts—

Though he later married, Ninetto was, for a time, Pasolini's lover.

(So I, turning my head in the gap,
like a screw driven from my mother into
the world, burst out, soundly and beautifully,
horrified and blue)—

Despite his passion for Ninetto, his nightly forays continued.

. . . After he left I kissed
the ghost of his body in the wrinkled whiteness.

And sometimes, in Rome and in Africa, his friends found him beaten, bleeding.

3 Family and Friends (Voice: Pasolini)

. . . In the thirties, a boy of sixteen
advised his brother
to defy the Duce, to join the Partisans. Their mother

was beautiful, almost a starlet; their father
a fascist who screamed at her for trifles:
a cracked glass, too much salt in the linguini . . .

She'd spit back that Mussolini
was a *culatta,* his big butt suited
for farts like him . . .

—Later, the brother, beautifully pure,
his face like the young Rimbaud, was blown apart
in the hills near Pisa. The father, a prisoner

half the war, returned, drunk, battered
by the defeat of his beloved
Duce. And the mother wept . . .

Soon the boy read Rimbaud: poems, like flares,
shot through his body. He touched himself in the cedars,
in the alleys of Casarsa. In sudden, alien

beautiful bodies. He grew darker. He survived . . .
There was no other way. I clapped my hands,
God vanished, and Eros appeared, goat and

goatherd, dancing, laughing, singing my desires.

—

Let me tell you how
this Sunday evening in the city
fills my soul

with a simple joy: Or
lamb cutlets *alla scottadito* (little
burned fingers):

Elsa, Alberto, Augusto,
Bertolluci, Bassani:
The gossip's

Fellini's new mistress; also, Laura's
supper last night where
Roberto rode her

rowdy bucking bronco.
When everyone left—I don't tell this to a soul—
she collapsed on the divan, tears

streaking mascara: "Why
do we grow older, Pa? My face is
crumbling." You're

more beautiful than ever, I lied.
(And left her after midnight
for my own concerns.)

. . . Strips of calamari, olive
oil and onions: Tell my ulcer I
won't stop. In the hospital I wrote six plays

and read Plato—my own
Purgatorio! . . . Later, I'll plummet
past this garden

to the city, the depths
below me, punks, pickpockets, whores
quickening the current. The waiter

shakes out a new tablecloth which
snaps flat and evening ends. Alberto
hands me a cigarette. I

breathe in. Something bursts
inside me. Contentment.
A smoky decay.

—

Having watched Ninetto saunter
off in the night ("Leave him go, Pa," I said to myself,
"he's simply restless . . ."), I

stumble home, pause: head swims:
Perhaps love, friendship,
should be impassive, impersonal.

I know nothing of Moravia's private life, nor he
of mine. It saves us from making
a mirror of the other, a narcissistic reflection . . .

With Ninetto? I can't stop. Like
any director, I *want* to subjugate, to block
his ego's light with the shadow of mine . . .

—I *am* a fool. Each time I see him
sneaking off to places I can't recall
(Oh, his innocent, blank, guilty look!),

I instantly forget: In this moment of history, this
self-consumed time, individual grief
rocks the gods

with consummate laughter . . .

4 *Trials*

A. Offenses

In October 1949, amid charges by his political adversaries, Pasolini was incriminated for "immoral acts involving juveniles." The facts were never proven: Pasolini was discharged for insufficient evidence. The young teacher did not deny something had happened. But he tried desperately to define the incident as an exotic literary experience, inspired by a recent reading of André Gide . . .

In 1955, on the publication of *Ragazzi di Vita,* a novel depicting the violence and amorality of life in the Roman slums, Pasolini entered the second of a series of trials which would never end, even with his death. Nearly all his films would be censored, denounced, and sued for crimes of obscenity, offenses against religion, and offenses against public morals . . .

B. The Court, The Circus, The Dream

"Ladies and gentlemen of this sandman circus,
this grubby, tiny press-stuffed hall, all crammed
with fascists, gossip queens, fairies, filmstars,
we charge this false *flâneur* of slums,
this so-called novelist,
blind, pornographic poet genius—
no, no, please hold your catcalls, your hot hisses—
(Please rise, Signore, to your confetti dream.)

"Oh now that the double-chinned Duce, our
forlorn and cue-balled, puppet Fascist Führer,
was righteously trashed by Partisan butchers,
stripping his sheep-in-wolf's war dress
from his cluck-cluck carcass,
all skewered, hung for wind and rain—

let's yank out a new whippet on a chain,
let's sell this big-top crowd a clown they crave!"

(I feel myself walking in, heavy gold chains
rattling on my neck. I shake them:
and suddenly I'm there, looking down on
the courtroom, the perspective

is God's or the angels' or a cloud's,
and there in the defendant's seat is
a tiny wooden puppet, its eyes bulging,
bloodshot, huge, and something sticking up

from its crotch, as if Pinocchio
had misplaced his nose, and every time
he struggles to speak, all that comes forth
is the clacking of his wooden teeth—)

" 'This,' Signore Pasolini proclaims, 'is
a cultural new wave!' *(a brief aside—*
To taste those spirochetes, syphilitic bits,
        of course, that's the true culture he craves)—
                Oh yes, yes, he protests,
        look how he flails his puppet staves!
How loudly he squeaks that we wield unjustly
our property, our power, the penis of history!—"

(Commotion. Shouts. Screeches.
Catcalls. Whistles. It seems myself, the puppet,
has suddenly fallen over to the floor,
the limbs flailing in an epileptic fit.)—

"Why listen to this shivering oak-brained farce?
Oh, I know, I know, he'll throw up Rimbaud,
hell-bent hyenas, slaves who won't kiss ass.
        Citing cretin Creon, he'll verse
                Antigone; then blow
        Gidean bubbles and Gramsci's nose—
Well, let him clatter. You can hear, it's all
shrieks, chokes and moans, a Chinese musical . . ."

(Now the puppet leaps to the table,
knocking a water glass; a guard with a night-
stick hacks wooden knees from under me,
and the puppet collapses in a shivering heap.

Hoots of laughter from the crowd, and
when I, the puppet, turn to look at them,
there's the face of my mother, a bruise
on her cheek, her tears blue and streaming.)—

"But let's peel back the petty charges,
that slashing of Italy's Papal pure pages:
Say sodomy butters each dish of love
        with creamy lips, that private hells
                our obedience dreams of
        in water closets, whispers, stairwells,
have devised this director, blow by blow—
Still other sins invoke the spotlight's glow—"

(I'M BLINDED I CAN'T SEE)—

“To seduce a boy, to ply him with wares,
(so Circe spelled, lured the lost to her lair),
to soothe those beatings by mother, by father,
  through touches, hot blue sighs and whispers,
    (Oh street-smart angel guise!),
  so that when he pulls up his eyes,
yes, moistened and trusting and full of terror,
there’s still a question that no one will answer—

    “Why am I so unworthy? devoid of love?—

“POWER, POWER, my friends, that’s what spits up
to hoist by his petard this pederast puppet:
How, through blindness to that battered boy’s eyes,
  this Marxist, this false Jesuit,
    abjures his own abandonment,
  proceeds by privilege over this
unequal in age, class, or intellect—
well, Signore, my brief ends abruptly thus:”

    (LIGHT LIGHT I CANNOT SEE) . . .

“You won’t wake up!”

5 *Intermission: Postcard from Rome*

I

Near the new train station in Rome, the great circle
where buses stagger in and out like exhausted beasts,
there, under plane trees, on benches, hot pots bubbling,

clutching bowls of rice, lifting chopsticks,
Cambodian refugees settle in for the evening
and ignore the gypsies: Pier, you'd have loved that contrast,

but what of me, my Japanese face, my American tongue,
my Mayflower wife, fighting our way off the Rebbibia bus?
And what of my rootless, jerry-built poem?

All through Italy we hunted you: That grove in Valvasone,
where you recited to your students Dante, Leopardi,
and dove cries threaded the cypress, and a creek gurgled

beneath the 12th century castle where Napoleon once slept.
And the banks of the Tiber, where we clambered over the fence,
down concrete steps cracked by weeds, poppies and punks,

and as the sludge brown waters trudged past, a father and son
gazed up from their fishing poles, smiled at our timid *buon giorno*.
But the slaughterhouses of Testaccio, the Trastevere slums,

or even the gangs of boys smoking beneath bridges?
They'd vanished like you into highrises, fine fabrics,
what you called the Neo-Capitalist dream. You, your rhetoric

and public shenanigans, your poems, your films, more
perishable than fashion. Irrelevant. Hysterical. "Pasolini?"
said our concierge. "Wasn't he that fag killed near Ostia?"

2

That day in Casarsa, with cicadas humming over fields
of wheat and maize, past roadside poppies, cypress, aleppo pine,
we came to a white-walled cemetery, rows of marble markers with

tiny oval pictures, names of some two dozen Colussi, your mother's
kin.
An old woman in kerchief puttered with her watering pail,
spotting the graves, refreshing roses, daisies, drooping jonquils.

Her face was dark, grizzled with fine white hairs, her figure
bleached by heat rising in waves from the white stone paths.
Suddenly Susie shouted. I rushed over. There, replacing your father,

as you had in life, next to the stone of Susanna, your mother,
was your grave—Pier Paolo Pasolini, 1922–1975—
in simple gray granite, nothing more. I stared

at your stone, the crisp brown baby's breath
in a battered brass vase. A nail-thin lizard shot like a minnow
across your name, where a monarch fluttered away

and tiny red chiggers kept wandering through the letters.
I was crying. I don't know why. Forgive me,
Pier, it seems so predictable . . .

3

Whatever lovely, unrepentant hymns you unfolded
to Christ or Marx, you were burdened by a frailty

you refused to acknowledge: how much
you were a disaster waiting to happen. Pier, in my country,

it's customary to ask why, why Pasolini?
We are young. We believe in the unconscious, an emotional life.

It's no good to say my genes are Japanese.
(I'll shave my head, study zen, answer a question with a question.)

No, let's be blunter than that—
We will never be intimate. Will always be the same.

Dear ghost, do not go to another house.

6 *Letter to Morante: the Pesaro Film Festival and Roland Barthes*

. . . I could not believe it. He *liked* my lecture, found
my linking of Godard's arhythmic cuts to
Brecht's Epic Theater, well, "useful." And yet

—I can't help it—I was disappointed. We were in the hotel
bar, leaning against leather chairs, hearing waiters
clatter across the marble (one looked like Ninetto

or so I wished). As I noted the way he balanced the
wineglass in his hand, his once thin face fleshed
out by casual feasts (sex for him must be merely

one more *petit déjeuner*), as I marked his absolutely
academic cardigan and tweed, despite our mutual
preference (he had a young student trailing

behind him like a page boy), I suddenly felt my boyhood
on the Po, the wheat fields and olive trees shoot up
between us, solid as a wall. And had this irrational

urge to shout: LOOK, LOOK AT THE DARKNESS, WHAT
WE ARE, WHAT EUROPE HAS BECOME! (Of course,
I did not. If I am the barbarian, the mutilating

drive towards rending and utopia: if each word,
each poem, authenticates each action; each action,
my life: if my negativity leaps beyond the pleasantries

of this author, his "The Death of the Author,"
i.e., if I believe in the soul and Barthes does not . . .) We stood
and kissed—which one Judas?—each other's cheek . . .

7 *Letter to Moravia*

Dear Alberto,

Nepal is mysterious, elusive, comforting.
Like a small child, our temple is propped
on the mountain's lap, and the snow at night
flows up the peaks, dark, earthly, and ghostly,
moonlight and white winds scraping the earth . . .

. . . Today, brushing my teeth, trying not to think
of Nino, I broke into this idiotic foam grin: Mad-
mirror scenes flashed through my brain: The Wife of Bath
tumbles from her mule, butt biting the dust;
or as Dante climbs the *Purgatorio* steps,
Virgil, who cannot pass to heaven, suddenly
sputters in childish pleasure, passing gas!

. . . Later I told a monk here about my films. They seemed,
to this bald Buddhist, carnivals of corruption—
pimps, punks and whores, the squawking Marxist crow
of *Hawks and Sparrows;* even the *Decameron* angels on the hill
spy like gray-stubbled grandpas on naked lovers.

. . . It's not just Ninetto I've lost. It's that boiling, run-amok
energy I shared once with delinquents, crooks and beggars.
Each time I watched the rich slide into taxis, I'd feel
this speechless rage, unlibeled by liberal tics.
And strolling down an alley, past sordid shadows
lounging in doorways, I'd think, here, here's
one I can talk to. Oh, I've still got my rage.
But that tense, claustrophobic intimacy . . .
(And yet I still let myself be dragged through
amoral interviews with *Le Monde* or *Oggi*.)

. . . I've come here like a stranger. I've slept with
no one. Just once not to pound out some bubble-thin
script, or the dull dogma nail, blunders of bad
carpenters and, what's worse, bad dialecticians.
Just hours without talking. Without thinking. Whiteness.
Blackness. Sleep.

Ciao, my friend. Your loving Pa.

8 *From the Pages of* Corriere della Sera *(Oct. 29, 1975): A Lutheran Letter*

. . . And what of the young, who were once my saviors?
Last week in Rome, two sixteen-year-olds with revolvers
shot their companion like Mafiosa thugs:
For money? No, his motorcycle's spark plugs.

And last night a fifteen-year-old fired a gun
at the legs of "a boy who practices nudism,"
then yelled: "Next time, I'll blast apart your mouth."
—The Papers of course leave such stories out.

Just as they ignore the Palace shenanigans,
deals with CIA, Mafiosi, bankers, oil firms:
These Christian Democrats slip favors to flatterers
just like the Bourbons, keeping proper manners.

And the public? When you are fooled a dozen times over . . .
And the Church? Merely a foreign financial power.
There's no copper in Italy, no ITT:
just missile bases in the hills of Tuscany.

(This isn't Chile. It's Christian Democrat Italy.)
Yes, in ten years, the petty bourgeoisie,
compulsory schools, a criminal TV,
have made their mockery of all I believed.

Let Calvino be Catholic, silent, deceived.
Let him scapegoat the well-bred Fascists of Parioli
whose murderous orgy in a villa one evening
is echoed each night by working-class punks all over Italy.

Look at the total, it's not aleatory:
In rage, in despair, I condemn our politic economy!
Hedonism, false tolerance, these are our deities.
Over and over I'll repeat my litany.

—Pier Paolo Pasolini

9 *A Violent Life*

On the evening of November 1, after dining with Ninetto Davoli and his family, Pasolini drove to the railroad station. There he invited a seventeen-year-old boy to take a ride with him . . .

Long ago, in the notes for my Oedipal film,
I wrote—
Think, think
of that first tableau, whether of Jocasta
begging her son, willing him not
to know, to question his existence,

or the scene before in which, coerced, caught,
abandoned in the climax of love, she
clamps her palm across his mouth, cutting

off his scream, or

Pini Pelosi, child of the slums, handsome, dim-witted, street crafty, former baker's boy, former café assistant, two-bit thief . . .

long after, when, from the rafters,
she hangs, naked, swaying, and he picks up the brooch,
the brooch he's unclasped, in tenderness, in lust, so many times,
and jabs its point

into his eyes,

there is, like the singing of Tiresias, like the blind,
stumbling Oedipus (led by some shepherd boy, some Ninetto),

always only one instant, a total
reading of the present, past, and future . . .

—So that choice, choice is not a

At 12:15 he and the boy were last seen at a filling station on the road to Ostia.

question: Say I try to see myself as
a leathery old man, lasting the years,
or a tidy, childless widow,

who sautés onions in olive oil, adding
oregano, basil, parsley; pasta that pours
from her kitchen whenever

a friend comes knocking, clutching
a manuscript, an empty bottle, a heart
like mine, broken like a stained-glass painting,
letting in magnificent light:
even if

When at 1:15, the police stopped a speeding car near the beach at Ostia they found a minor at the wheel. They guessed the car was stolen . . .

I wanted—and I do not—

to stop these prowlings, kneelings
in the damp grass, staining my jeans, wind
dried sperm sticky on skin, obscure

openings to pleasure or pain; yes, even if

At dawn near a soccer field and a settlement of shacks, his body was found, beaten, his heart crushed by tires. Pelosi's ring lay next to it . . .

I wanted to heed their warnings,

Alberto, Laura (sweet, sweet Jaguar), my
own lost son, Ninetto, how—it is
not possible—
                                        could I ever stop? Everywhere I walk, past
the shops, the boulevards, the riches of Rome,

nihilism, the panther, crouches
at each branch, descends

on the infinite . . . Somehow

On Italian state television, that same day, the homosexual aspects of Pasolini's life and death were dwelt on exclusively . . .

I've lost the fog-brushed valley where,
as a child on the Po, I was mad for April's

green, fall glistening olives, soaked
in the Friulian dialectical hills . . .

The whole affair could be shrugged off as just another typical end of a queer.

—A poem to fuck Fascism, yes, that's what I dreamed!

10 A Fascist Death, A Purgatorial Dream

(*Ditate:* the exchange of blows with extended index and middle fingers; Pasolini spoke of playing this game with boys till blood came.)

Lured on by *lire* to this drought-dazed field,
he bounces off the hood and laughs and smears his
forearm with your blood. (Isn't it a kick, Pa, this
double digits, a slap, a cut?) As he strains the bit,
his muscles, bellowing, blow out your body,
which stiffens, crumples, greets his grunts with airy
moans: like a cell dividing,
something inside you's breaking, driving,
thump, thump, each muffled blow: his kneecap stuns
your groin; hemorrhage, pain, blackness drums.

Or say, at this point, that the scene transposes—
A Fiat drives up, three men in sunglasses,
in Milano leather. One shouts, shoves the trick
(But hasn't he done it, just what they asked?);
one lights a cigarette, slides it between
the boy's lips, as he inhales, quivering;
one grabs the keys. Your Romeo crawls
towards you, crushes your skull . . .

Or: as covenant to the earth's breath ruffling
your hair, there, in the dark, a boy—is it me?—
kneels, presses his lips to yours. He
hears bats flicker like stuttering tongues,
a whistling night-flight and rat-wing, blood-touch;
and the night who loved you, minister to wandering
strangers, shivers, recalls the boys scrawling
in the dirt the body desire, fist that punishes
pleasure, deeper, deeper, that tells the world:
I will this knowledge, this
bleeding, byzantine farewell.

Or: this kiss—

11 An Epitaph for Pier Pasolini (1922–1975): Open & Shut

Here is the rose of history. Pull the petals apart.
A faint murmuring starts, then shouting, shrieking,
an interminable roar. So you close the rose, call it
simple, a rose without history, innocent, eternal.

III

Now that they must know more, the poets have become angry.

—ELIAS CANETTI

THE ARCHITECT'S SON

All night was the smell of mint
and as the father said Jamie
it's time to say good-bye to the world
even as the boy's eyes opened a second
a space in the dark as wide as constellations
there was the nurse slipping out the needle of
morphine and the body turning blue and
brittle and black like bark like
something that grew from the earth
and had roots a hundred feet beneath the surface
everywhere beneath the house

in the morning down the hill
the squatters got up from the sidewalk
and the all-night diner turned off its neon
and the Hmong and Vietnamese mothers
came home from the hushed buildings
or set out shopping for bok-choy rice or milk
and their clothes ill-sorted ill-fitting
fluttered a little
when they opened their doors

and walking with no purpose past buildings
that would stand forever in the photos of his time
what the father could not help bring back
was the daily battles of Demerol and pain
how the boy twisted his face like a demon's mask
screeched at the nurses spit at the resident
plunging needle after needle in the punctured veins

it is difficult to wait for love or fame or death
and the city keeps its own cruelty
as we keep ours
and the mothers wash their doorsteps with a little blood
to keep away demons
or sweep away dust with battered brooms
while factory smokestacks start pouring their white heaps
in the morning sun (back at the house
a wife no longer his would be waiting to start
the calls announcing that end as simple
as smoke as an apple falls)

just then a beautiful woman her red hair a corona in the sun
walked towards him as quickly as politeness would allow
and she was already behind him
when like a hand raised to wave
he discovered ashamed and bewildered
his desire to speak

he was forty his son five
who had slit his body open
and slipped a cloud inside
just as in the last story
the boy made up
explaining how the river gulls fly

LE VICE-CONSUL—OR: DURAS

The beginning is murky, like the Cardamom hills.
The beggar woman not really a woman,
but a child, a child with child,
stumbles on a gravel pit. Abandoned.
Has followed the birds past nightfall.

The outskirts of Pursat, among the thousands,
old toothless men, beggars, simpletons (—later
will come the soldiers, young wiry boys,
eyes of emptiness and red bandanas,
boys from the highlands, villages like hers);

and now she joins them, bearded women,
bird women, women who drift sluggishly
near the banks, turning to stones, silver scaled fish.
Around her are shadows, smoky fires. She sleeps.
Vomits. Sleeps. There's hunger in her belly, a mouth,

a hand like a fin, a face like a reptile, curled
inward, drifting inside her, in the current
near shore. Where is the Plain of Birds? It starts
to rain. She starts to dream . . . She smells the soup
vendors, their steaming garlic, stands by the white

house, where bowls of steaming rice are left
on the steps. And the nibbling in her belly ceases.
Fires on the plain, memory, ceases. She
stares at the river's current. A dead pig floats by.
A log. A face. A feeling. Her mouth is dry.

She has no child, just a swollen belly, an
overstretched drum. Salt, smoke, mud. These
are the tastes on her tongue. Soon she will follow

the birds. She will forget this year, this day;
find herself in another continent. There

a French woman is writing of an embassy ball,
a figure on a balcony, a sail on the river;
in the alley, as the heat of evening settles,
a beggar woman stumbles down the cobbles,
singing in an unknown language. This is her song.

HUY NGUYEN: BROTHERS, DROWNING CRIES

1

Shaking the snow from your hair, bowl-cut
like an immigrant's, you hand me your assignment—
Compare and Contrast. Though your accent stumbles
like my grandfather's, you talk of Faulkner,
The Sound and the Fury. You mention Bergson,
whom you've read in French. *Durée*. How the moment lasts.
Your paper opens swimming the Mekong Delta.

2

As you lift your face, the sun flashes
down wrinkles of water; blue dragonflies
dart overhead. You hear your brother call.
You go under again, down, down, till you
reach the bottom, a fistful of river clay,
mold a ball in the dark, feel your lungs struggle,
waiting to burst—

Where is your brother?

Against the current's thick drag, stumble
to shore, the huts of fishermen—
My brother, my brother's drowned!

Faces emerge from black doorways,
puzzled, trotting towards you, then
all of them running to the river,
diving and searching the bottom
not for clay but flesh,

and there the man

crawls up on the beach, your brother
slumped over his shoulder, bouncing up
and down as the man runs up and down,
water belching from your brother's mouth
but no air, no air: flings
your brother to the ground, bends,
puts mouth to your brother's lips,
blows in, blows out, until your brother's
chest expands once, once, and once,
and his eyes flutter open, not yet back
in this world, not yet recognizing the blue
of the sky, that your people see as happiness,
even happier than the sun.

3

Five years since you drifted on the South China Sea,
and the night Thai pirates sliced your wife's finger for
a ring, then beat you senseless. You woke to a merchant ship
passing in silence, as if a mirage were shouting for help.
Later, in that camp in Bataan, loudspeakers told
of a boat broken on an island reef, and the survivors
thrashing through the waves, the tide pulling out,
and the girl who reached the shore and watched
the others, one by one, fall from starvation,
as she drank after each rain from shells on the beach.
At last only her brother remained, his eyes staring
upwards at the wind and the sun, calling her name . . .
The camp went silent, then a baby, a woman sobbing.
And you knew someone was saved to tell the story.

4

Now, through Saigon, your mother carries kettles of soup to
sell at dawn.
While malaria numbs your brother's limbs, he shivers on a
cot in prison.
You write: "I wait for his death. Safe. Fat. World away." I
red mark your English.
There was a jungle you fought in. There's a scar above your
wrist.
A boy dives, splashes and, going down, clutches his stomach
and twists.
You're at the bus stop by Target. Snow still falling, a fine
blown mist.

LAN NGUYEN: THE UNIFORM OF DEATH (1971)

At the jungle's edge, torn open
near the neck, the carcass of a dog.
Five hissing flies bathe in the wound.
Brush them away and tiny white worms
swim like grains of rice in a soup
of blood. I hack off the head.

At night, in a row down the road, a hundred heads.
Dust swirls around them, little whirlwinds,
and I hear the heads breathing,
humming indecipherable murmurs, a foreign tongue.
They stop: a high scream like a woman's—

My hand's at my mouth
to clamp it shut.

In the river, my face
is twisted, mottled green,
a mango rotted eight days in the jungle's oven.
I splash the water, wait to clear.

Only water, only water.

Where is the man's face I dragged to the fire?
Through his screams, I saw skin bubble and blacken.
Ground the head down farther, felt flames
hiss at my wrists, let go—
It fell with a thump, sparks jumped, I
held them in my palm.

Licking my fingertips,
I smelled his face.

Cutting sliver after sliver
from the branches of bamboo,
we fashioned a cage for crickets.
They sang each night
beside a jar of fireflies.
When my brother knocked them from the table,
they spread out like sparks of a flare
before the copters darted down river,
wings beating . . .

Flares, fireflies, flares, fireflies . . .

If you cut its legs, a cricket,
since it sings from its legs,
just rocks, silent on its belly;
but tear each limb from his sockets,
a man still sings out with a burst of his lungs.

I think we should fight underwater,
crawling at the river bottom,
moving heavily, flies caught in honey.
Always, no matter how much blood
oozes out in murky clouds, no matter how
the faces freeze in the last gulp
for air, no matter how much you want
to mourn, your brother in your hands,
nothing cries out—only the thick thunder
of the current moves in your ears.

Not with a light tap on the shoulder
but with a tiny cylinder of lead
hurled so fast it knocks a man flat,

I mark men unfit for life;
so many, I ask the figure
who will call me from life—
Who is the impostor?
Who wears the uniform of death?

HOPE WITHOUT HOPE

Words on the page, prayers, even shouts of rage,
What do they count against tanks, missiles, guns?
For each line that you write, each war you wage,
Ten thousand hands write reams to drown your one.

No matter how beautiful, pungent, pure,
In that cacophony, your poems are like roses
Tossed on an ocean of thunderous azure;
Washed in the gutter by a dozen hoses.

Okay then. Nothing could be more utterly
Useless. History rolls on, lie by lie.
You, in a world of greed and cruelty,
Who offer us poems, well, tell me. Why? Why?

THE BOOKSTORE

He keeps them in the closet. In piles. In years.
There are some with slick glossy pages, the faces of cheerleaders
or debutantes, his students at the college. Sometimes
the paper is cheaper, the color awry, and the women
have the look of someone who's been used, who's escaped from
Fargo or Farmington, her makeup too thick and pointed, bearing her
class.
(He meets her in the saunas on Lake Street, the stage of the Faust.)
Their poses are improbable and promising, no flesh is hidden.
It is late afternoon, sounds of the freeway drift through the room.
His wife is working, she will not see him.
He is tired. He may or may not know he is depressed.
He goes to the closet. He rummages through the piles,
looking for one that will spark him, that will let him go.
Through the hundreds of magazines, not one can satisfy . . .

He drives through stoplights, his mouth clamped on a joint.
Into a parking lot. Pulls in beside the spray-painted scrawl—
"Porn Hurts Women." Rushing past, he enters
a room with peeling green paint cracks, fluorescent lights,
cracked linoleum tiles, rubbed deep with dirt. Plywood racks
of *Oui, Playboy, Penthouse, Swedish Erotica, The Angel Series,*
anonymous issues of leather and bondage. He does not look
at the clerk, a young boy with bowl-cut hair and pimples, a dragon
tattoo exposed by his sleeveless T-shirt. Picking up the magazines
wrapped in plastic, the man tries to guess by the covers
what lies inside. Never quite sure, stoned, he takes
nearly an hour to make his choice. He takes one
up to the counter. Then brings it back. It isn't right.
He asks for quarters. Heads back to the video booths.

The booths are painted black, also made of plywood.
On each door is a display with stills from the movies inside.
He goes from door to door, eyeing each one, trying
not to look at the gays, who lean in the corners, key chains
clinking, a cigarette or toothpick dangling from their mouths.
He is looking for the perfect film, the blonde that will stun
him with her moans, the whimpering that sets off a trembling inside
    him,
released by a cock of monstrous proportions, which dwarfs
his own with envy, with the certainty that only here,
here in this booth, its damp sticky floor, its private dark,
can he possess this image, let it consume his life.
He unzips his pants and slips in the quarter.
The reel rolls, music and moaning, ending abruptly.
Five minutes. Another quarter. Five minutes. Another quarter.
Again, again, from booth to booth, the hour slips by.
He does not want to come. He wants to hold it, the tensions,
as long as he can. He leaves the store with three magazines
which he cannot help but begin unwrapping in the car.
He stops himself. He knows he needs to nurse their charge.
One time through and he will need another. He drives home
with one hand on himself.

                    Up in his bedroom, he undresses,
spreads the magazines on the bed, lies beside them.
He studies each image, noting their position, the expression
on their face. He reads the captions, how the women tell
the men how they want it, how they can't get enough.
He is still trying hard not to come.

An hour later
he hears his wife drive up. He picks up the magazines,
his pants, runs to the washroom, worried she will find
him, angered by her arrival, disrupting his peace.
He will rush his orgasm. He will not feel satisfied.
He will feel the hours he has wasted, the shame emerging.
He will say he needs to take a shower.
The magazines are in the bathroom. Already

they are not enough.

LOST IN THE PHILIPPINES

FOR MY FATHER

1 Northern Luzon: A Dream

Bound for the terraced
rice fields of Banaue, stranded,
no jeepney till dawn,
in a browned-out mountain town,
I matched beers with two civil guards:
as their faces floated into
blackness, as the night crept in,
I saw a look ancient, Indian,
and thought I was lost in the Andes
and would never get back. I
got back, and slept that night
in Enrique's house, listened
to his mother-in-law complain
about no respect for authority,
about human rights, and when I
woke with two hands smothering
my mouth, I knew I would die
like a dog, choking and squealing, robbed
for my weakness and American sins.
But it was only the blueness of a
cock's crow, the hot glistening
touch of my wacky paranoia,
and beneath a huge portrait of
Ferdinand and Imelda, I fell back to
sleep, recalling your face, rippling
down my body, shuddering in
affection, a pure white dream.

2 *Visions of* **Dharama**

Once in a cold green office, amid a cluster of photos
—river, cane fields, a child of Negros, the bloated body—
a woman's cigarette burned to a long finger of ash,
and when the night and neon of Tokyo flooded the window,
I, like a fool, wondered why Lut's taut, dark face still bloomed
with a stream of rage, the hours and years of her island,
till she was no longer young, no longer beautiful,
and the century was still closing like a damp, dark wound.

Later, past the rusted tin shacks of squatters, past children
waving and wading waist high in monsoon sewage,
I stumbled on the great trash heaps of Manila, smoking in the rain
(there scavengers pick their living three shifts a day).
That night, a girl stepped from a doorway, sporting
a Madonna T-shirt, a plastic gold chain. Fresh from street craps
and sniffing glue, giggling the five Japanese words she possessed,
she tugged my arm. I blushed, stammered, hurried away.

Today, after wandering past jade trees, Kyoto's stone gardens,
by the golden temple, I sat reading of Marcos, Imelda's high heels,
the sacking of Malacañang. Lut has gone back: "Cory comes
from the oligarchy . . . Still, I have hope." I thought of Asia—
gooks, mongols, slant-eyed slopes; coolies, sarongs, *ao dais,*
Filipinos, tumbling to the future, spilt like tea on a silk kimono,
staining a whiteness preserved for years. And me? Just a tourist,
I heard them whisper: "*Bakka, boi-chan,* get on with your life!"

THE ONE WHO TELLS, THE ONE WHO BURNS

(Soweto)

An evening haze on the hills, on the rusted tin hutches,
yards cluttered with bicycles, cans, chicken-wire cages;
laundry drooping in the halfhearted wind. These aren't the homelands.
Is this my home? I chomp down on the sandwich, the sky hunches
over me, and I think this growling in my stomach, it will cease . . .

That day I entered the office I would not let go
my hat, I held it like a flag in front of my genitals.
My head was bowed and quiet, as if at prayer, and it felt
like my first time in one of those houses, when I faced that woman,
that one time I had money among the many I did not.
And the man said quick and cold, *wait here,* and I sat
on the bench, stared at the President on the wall, at the fan whirring
and clacking, at the clock, the clerk pushing back spectacles on a nose
bulbed like a tomato, rooted in the pocked white flesh . . .

I take a sip of warm beer, spit in the dirt. I don't want
to sleep. A redness rises from the edges of the plains,
blood on the borders of night. On the road a dog trots up,
tail wagging, but there's something funny, there's
only three legs sputtering in the dust . . .

There was a cardboard box, the kind for refrigerators.
And one end was stripped. I entered its darkness.
The box was cool and hot all at once. I peered through the slit.
Is that the man? Yes. That's the man. (How simple it was!)
And I recalled the bullhorn, the crowds, the gravel road,
how the trees were behind him, throwing their long
shadows over us, and they were swaying like dancers,
in rhythm to the words. He shouted louder. The crowd shouted,
clapped;

I shouted and clapped. (Now I don't, can't, recall a word.)
And then I walked out of the box. And they handed me my money.

And today on the streets where the kids scratched
figures in the dirt, where boys dribbled a ball back and forth,
where men, sleep in their eyes, lined up, stepped into the bus,
and the women waddled past with bundles on their heads,
today on the streets where that three-legged mongrel trotted,
they surrounded him, not the mongrel, what they did
was too horrible for a mongrel. Hoisting the man aloft,
they ringed his body with tires, so that he grew slats,
like a light bulb, and where the bulb should have been,
were only his eyes, wild and helpless,
and the crowd shouted for oil, the torch, the fire to be.
When I looked up at him, caught in the crowd, he,
like a diamond, caught my eye: and his look said, Brother . . .

I lie back in the dust of this hill, feel the sky press down
the weight of night. The money is gone, my belly full.
And now like a flag I'm waiting to be unfurled . . .

IV

In the end hope, wrested from reality by negating it, is the only form in which truth appears. Without hope, the idea of truth would be scarcely even thinkable, and it is the cardinal untruth, having recognized existence to be bad, to present it as truth simply because it has been recognized.

—THEODOR ADORNO

GRANDFATHER-IN-LAW

It's nothing really, and really, it could have been worse, and of course,
he's now several years dead,
and his widow, well, if oftentimes she's somewhat distracted, overly
cautious when we visit—
after all, Boston isn't New York—she seems, for some reason, enormously
proud that there's now a writer in the family,
and periodically, sends me clippings about the poet laureate, Thoreau,
Anne Sexton's daughter, Lowell, New England literary lore—
in which I fit, if I fit at all, simply because I write in English—as if color
of skin didn't matter anymore.
Still, years ago, during my first visit to Boston, when we were all asleep,
he, who used to require that my wife memorize lines of Longfellow or
Poe and recite them on the phone,
so that, every time he called, she ran outdoors and had to be coaxed back,
sometimes with threats, to talk to Pops
(though she remembers too his sly imitations of Lincoln, ice cream at
Brighams, burgers and fries, all the usual grandfatherly treats),
he, who for some reason was prejudiced against Albanians—where on
earth did he find them I wondered—
who, in the thirties, would vanish to New York, catch a show, buy a suit,
while up north,
the gas and water bills pounded the front door (his spendthrift ways
startled me with my grandfather's resemblance),
who for over forty years came down each morning, "How's the old goat?"
with a tie only his wife could knot circling his neck,
he slipped into my wife's room—we were unmarried at the time—and
whispered so softly she thought
he almost believed she was really asleep, and was saying this like a wish
or spell, some bohunk miscalculated Boston sense of duty:
"Don't make a mistake with your life, Susie. Don't make a mistake . . ."
Well. The thing that gets me now, despite the dangling rantings I've let
go, is that, at least at that time,
he was right: There was, inside me, some pressing, raw unpeeled persis-
tence, some libidinous desire for dominance

that, in the scribbled first drafts of my life, seemed to mark me as wastrel and rageful, bound to be unfaithful,
to destroy, in some powerful, nuclear need, fissioned both by childhood and racism, whatever came near—
And I can't help but feel, forgiving him now, that if she had listened, if she had been awake,
if this flourishing solace, this muscled-for-happiness, shared by us now, had never awakened,
he would have become for me a symbol of my rage and self-destruction, another raw, never healing wound,
and not this silenced grandfatherly presence, a crank and scoundrel, red-necked Yankee who created the delicate seed of my wife, my child.

ELEGY FOR A POET

FOR JOHN MACOUBRIE

You could not come back any older or sadder
So this icy March morning
Brought you to my window with your hair still brushed
Across the bald spot on your skull
And bits of Kleenex patched on your cheek
Where you had cut yourself shaving

Better this than the flesh discolored like bark
Pressed against a hospital pillow
For more than a year your marrow had failed
To produce more blood
Until at last a fungus began to grow absence
In your brain, little pockets
Where thoughts vanished and connections failed

Still I read you the last night
From the *Four Quartets*
And your hand felt soft and weightless
Like a dream as you mumbled
From time to time echoing
The lines

Sirens rose from the street then passed
The nurse came and changed your IV
The resident came and drew your blood
The *Quartets* moved on

John there must be this goodness in death
That makes us love the dead so much

THE EMERGENCY ROOM

Note: Stab. *(long* a*) is short for* stabilization

You were just a med student then,
and as evenings grew dark and scattered with stars,
you'd return from the County coiled tight, straight
from the trenches, drugged by the lack of sleep:
"At ten a stab. case came in. The woman was moaning
(she'd been found behind the 7-Eleven).
David, half of her skull had been crushed in,
her whole left side paralyzed. She
was naked from the waist down . . .
No, they didn't catch him. And no one knows
who she is. I just hope she wasn't conscious.
They thrust tubes down her throat, her nose,
IV's in her body, and left her stripped, exposed
on the table, while the doctors and nurses gathered
their instruments. It was like another assault.
I sat there and wrote it down, instrument by
instrument, procedure by procedure, cut by cut
. . . Now? If she's lucky, she won't wake up . . ."

Later, down in Arkansas, they picked him up,
brought him back for trial. Barely
literate, a black ex-con. On TV, in a brief clip,
his face looked hollowed, haggard, his teeth
gapped and twisted, his eyes dead. It was as if
he'd become a thing like stones or dust,
sand or salt, his soul a net full of shadows.
I felt unnerved, fatuous, somehow responsible . . .

And the victim? Beneath the covers, shivering
almost unconsciously, you left her for another,
her story spilling out—
                                        "That wasn't all. At two
a woman came in with her blouse torn open,

her skirt in shreds. She was in shock.
Gradually I got her story out: From the age
of before she could remember, she had been raped
by her father. David, I couldn't believe it:
She was thirty-four . . . Finally, she moved
across the river, came to the city only for therapy:
This time her father was waiting. He chased her down 94,
forced her to the side of the road and walked her
into the woods and tied her to a tree . . ."

Silence. You sat up, pulled your knees to your chest.
Asked for water.
                                        "He tried again and again. He kept
holding his limp penis, pressing it against her.
In rage, he began to stuff mud up her vagina,
at the same time, whipping her thighs with a pine branch.
This went on from late afternoon to long after sunset . . .
After she finished, I didn't know what to say. I just cried.
She, she seemed startled. Relieved . . ."

Susan, what can I say? Some part of me
knows that man? What *do* I know? Even then
I knew I'd never comprehend how the rapist,
the incestuous father, his almost inhuman rage,
that could crush so endlessly his will to love,
enters, like a messenger, a woman's existence.
And yet—God, is this why I'm telling this?—
I felt jealous. You had witnessed these stories . . .

It's years later. A friend tells me of writing on the Holocaust,
spending night after night in the office of Himmler,
in visions of ash and the crystals of gas: how the desire arose
to rub each entrenched, lime-drenched body against the reader's

psyche and skin. And then on a trip to Dachau,
she was there, shaking, holding her palm to the brick
of the ovens, feeling the weight of those voices, those faces,
those spirits push against her, enfold her, a presence
as palpable as a violent wind; and yet it was only when
she walked through those gates—"Work Sets You Free"—emblazoned
above,
and walked down the hill to a small sapling,
surrounded by pink, blushing petunias, only then
was she able to sit and rest and let it out,
the only answer annealed to that earthly beauty—
"I knew that I couldn't write it with just Himmler, the camps,
the corpses, there had to be more, these moments of release"—
a clarity of tears, sunlight; the aimless, unfolding
hills; a sapling, petunias, bending in the breeze.

THIS LOSS, THIS BRIGHTNESS

1

As I knead your back, the lotion melding with sweat beads, clusters of
birthmarks, their small constellations, you begin
your nightly recitation of Code Blues and tiny stretchered bodies. Tonight
I'm haunted like a child by your story of this girl, Daneesha
Brown:
How, in a room sealed in whiteness, fluorescent lights, you bend to the
bed and lift her fresh-burned hand, unpeel the bandage
and pause just a moment, to let her, you, the wound breathe. But the
mocha skin keeps oozing an ashen black,
crumbling the way leprosy might, and no antibiotic, through the glistening
IV's, can unwither what's obviously dying . . .
"There was nothing more to do. The surgeons set up shop . . . both hands
and feet came off . . ."
And then she is back, wheeled in by orderlies, this bundled bedded body,
braided hair straddling her face, cells collapsing in fever,
breath veering to evanescence, lines, intubations, a mélange of drugs—
"I've never worked so hard to keep one alive"—
As you lead me through your night, each hour a victory, a staving off of
defeat, you turn and I see this brightness, like the exhalation
of a falling star,
flow through your face, still threading the ward corridors, before sleep
sets in: "We made it. We got her out . . ."

2

Madeline's adopted daughter, Mira, whirls at the corner and points—
"Carz, tru, streeee . . ."
As she chases peek-a-boo around the oak with you, her face so dark, so
deliciously alert, we both recall her at five months,
still only five pounds, a small pale sugar sack you could place in your palm,
and think of the teeming, dusty New Delhi streets, incense-scented sheets
that spawned her,

her mother settling in exhaustion and heat, the little homunculi spinning
inside her, flinging the stream, one-in-a-million-chance destination . . .
Back at the party, amid talk of the hearings on TV, you ask Madeline
what's been most difficult in this adopted single parenthood.
She pauses for moments, minutes, before coming in—the question politely
almost forgotten—
"It's what she arouses in me . . . love . . . need . . . affection . . . I'm surprised by how strongly I feel,
and it's great, but at times it tells me I'm missing something, adult
reciprocation, another answer to that gap I feel . . ."
And we, the married, nod, as if understanding, and the talk turns back to
the contras, Iran, that bastard Reagan . . .
That night, the egg we fertilized was flushed from the moist womb lining;
blood, meant for creation,
spilt for nothing, a tiny bit of sadness and waste. Dripping from the
shower, your head, your body wrapped in white towels,
you sprawled yourself on the bed, looked up at the ceiling. I lay down
beside you (the ceiling would do as well as the stars).
"Oh there are hormones and other drugs with magic," you said, "but
magic, we've lived so much of our lives on magic . . ."
You talked of Daneesha, the way her amputations kept coming. How each
day she rose up smaller,
angrier, inconsolable: "They can't cut more," she'd say, "they promised . . . there's nothing left . . ." She simply couldn't *believe*
what was happening.
"David," you said, "how can we keep thinking we'll be so lucky . . ."

3

At La Cucina tonight I told Madeline and Joann how it took two tries
to pour it in the bottle (where but in *Portnoy* would you ever
try to aim?);

you couldn't help but add, ". . . his sperm tested plentiful but—good feminist—lacked aggression." Then somewhere between the *prima* and *secondi,*
Joann trashed the Salle show at the Walker, and you finished your story of Daneesha Brown.
Through three weeks, each time you entered, she never seemed to know you—it's hard, with the masks;
you're just an eerie, gauze-white presence—and in her room a last time, your rotation over,
you tell her gently, thinking it won't matter, "I'm not going to be your doctor anymore."
But from that small, whittled-away body, there bolted a shriek, some high, penetrating question, "Why do you have to go? Why? Why?"
Leaning to the table, you let her cry brush the candle flame and light over us, and there was no way to take it in: instead I saw,
for an instant, your face in the future, some ten, twenty years from now—how did it happen? will there be children?
so much faith and foolishness our only armor—you were concentrated, radiant, so utterly beautiful.

NOTES

"Grandfather and Grandmother in Love"—*Biwa:* a Japanese stringed instrument. *Otoo-san:* father; *okaa-san:* mother (Japanese couples call each other Father and Mother). *Ran:* chaos.

"The *Hibakusha*'s Letter (1955)"—*Utskemono:* Japanese pickles.

"An Argument: On 1942"—*Shoyu:* soy sauce. *Furoshiki:* a scarf that is used to carry things. *Mochi:* rice cakes. *Benjo:* toilet.

"Suite for Grandfather and Grandmother Uyemura: Relocation"—*Obi:* the sash of a kimono. *Hakujin:* literally "white people." *Udon:* Japanese noodles. *Tatami:* straw mats.

"A *Nisei* Picnic: From An Album"—*Nisei:* second-generation Japanese Americans. The phrase *Shikatta ga nai* (It can't be helped) encapsulates a very fundamental Japanese attitude.

"Song for Uncle Tom, Tonto and Mr. Moto"—*Hana:* a Japanese card game.

"Pasolini"—*Gospel:* Pasolini's film *The Gospel According to St. Matthew. Sodom:* the film *Salo: The 120 Days of Sodom.* Friulian: Friuli is the section of Italy to the northeast of Venice, where Pasolini spent much of his youth and where his mother's hometown, Casarsa, is located.

On the deaths of Barthes and Pasolini: Barthes's was absurd, almost comical—struck in the street by a laundry truck (a misreading of signs?); Pasolini's a mélange of politics, sexuality, and melodrama—killed by a trick in a soccer field, or made to appear so, hiding the designs of fascists in the self-destruction of his desires. Did Pasolini believe he was evil? Yes. No. Did he believe the society he lived in was evil? Yes. No . . . Yes, no, yes, no —Isn't that the way he lived his life?

To view Pasolini's life in terms of sexual addiction is, of course, a reduction. Not to do so is to sentimentalize the urges of self-destruction (as well as to miss how well he imbibed, consciously or unconsciously, the morals of Italy: Homosexual = Outlaw).

Two quotations served as talismans for this poem. The first was Valéry's pronouncement: "Europe will be punished for its politics; it will be deprived of its wines, its beer and liqueurs. And of other things." —A remark that first struck me as absolutely accurate, and now, after writing this poem, dated, almost naïve. The second quotation is from Walter Benjamin: "It goes without saying that photography is unable to say anything about a power station or a cable factory other than this: what a beautiful world!" In various ways, Pasolini kept asking, What does this remark mean for the art of our time?

"Lost in the Philippines"—Malacañang: the presidential palace of the Philippines; here Imelda Marcos kept, among other things, several thousand pairs of shoes. *Bakka:* idiot or dumbbell (slang). *Boi-chan:* little boy. Negros: an island in the Philippines.

"This Loss, This Brightness"—In some residency programs, residents switch hospitals after a six- or eight-week period.

ABOUT THE AUTHOR

David Mura, a third generation Japanese-American or *sansei*, has published poems in *The Nation, The American Poetry Review, Crazyhorse, The New Republic,* and *The Missouri Review,* and has written a book, *A Male Grief: Notes on Pornography and Addiction*. His essays have appeared in the *Partisan Review,* the *Threepenny Review,* and the *Graywolf Annual Five Multicultural Literacy*. He has been the recipient of many awards and fellowships, one of which enabled him to study in Japan. David Mura lives with his wife, Susan Sencer, a pediatrician, in St. Paul.